Level 4 is ideal for children who are ready to read longer stori~~~ and are eager to start read~~~

Special features

Clear type

Full, exciting story

Corporal Pig saw his chance. The bird guarding the nest had gone to sleep! The pigs grabbed all three eggs and made off with them.

King Pig was going to be so pleased!

Richer, more varied vocabulary

Longer sentences

There were one or two things that Stella was going to need. First, she pulled up a big weed. Then she grabbed an old shawl. Without explaining, she set off for the slingshot.

Detailed illustrations to capture the imagination

Educational Consultant: Geraldine Taylor
Book Banding Consultant: Kate Ruttle

A catalogue record for this book is available from the British Library

This edition published by Ladybird Books Ltd 2014
80 Strand, London, WC2R 0RL
A Penguin Company

001

ISBN: 978-0-72328-908-1

Printed in China

STELLA AND THE EGG TREE

Written by Richard Dungworth
Illustrated by Ilias Arahovitis

In Pig City, all was not well.
King Pig was in a bad mood.
And when King Pig was in a bad
mood, it was very bad news for
all the other pigs!

"Where are my eggs?" King Pig asked Corporal Pig. "You must have them for me by now!"

Corporal Pig went red and looked down.

"No?" said the king. "WHY NOT?" he yelled.

"It's those rotten birds, Your Majesty," explained Corporal Pig. "They guard their nest so well, day and night. We just can't get to their eggs!"

King Pig looked furious. "Are you telling me that you can't deal with one or two silly little birds?" he yelled. "Get out of here and don't come back without my eggs!"

12

13

Later that day, on the other side of Piggy Island...

Red, Chuck, Bomb and the Blues were playing ball. Stella was looking after the eggs. The sun was out and it was making Stella feel a little sleepy.

Corporal Pig saw his chance.
The bird guarding the nest had gone
to sleep! The pigs grabbed all three
eggs and made off with them.

King Pig was going to be so pleased!

Stella was NOT pleased. "The eggs!"
she cried. "They've gone!"
The other birds came over.
"The pigs must have taken them,"
said Red furiously.
"What do we do about it?"
said Chuck.

"Not 'we', Chuck," said Stella. She was just as furious as Red. "It's up to me to put things right. I'll get our eggs back. No rotten pig gets away with playing a trick on me!"

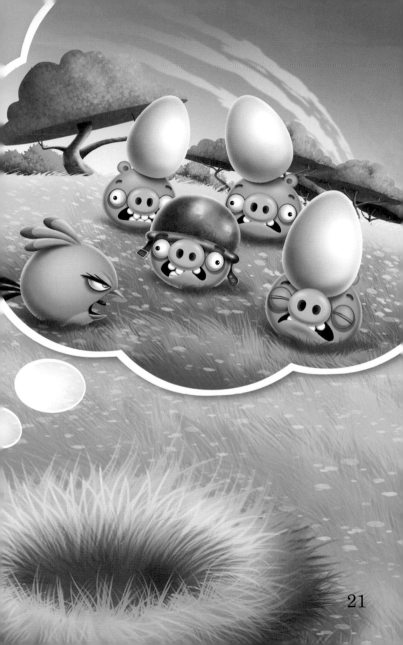

There were one or two things
that Stella was going to need.
First, she pulled up a big weed.
Then she grabbed an old shawl.
Without explaining, she set off
for the slingshot.

The pigs were well on their
way back to Pig City when
they met a stranger. She was
an odd-looking old pig in a shawl.

"Well, my pigs!" she cried.
"Where are you going?"

Corporal Pig was only too
pleased to tell the stranger
his good news.

"We're going back to Pig City,
to see King Pig," he said.
"We have eggs for him –
three big eggs!"

"I'm sure King Pig will be pleased to have them!" said the old pig. "But only three? Is that all? It seems odd to take only three eggs, when King Pig could have as many as he likes!"

Corporal Pig looked at the stranger. "As many as...? But how...?" he said.

The old pig laughed. "I will tell you – for a price!" she said. "But we have no way to pay you," said Corporal Pig.

"You can pay me with an egg," said the stranger. "For just one egg, I will tell you how to get as many more as you like."

The pigs thought this seemed like a very good deal.

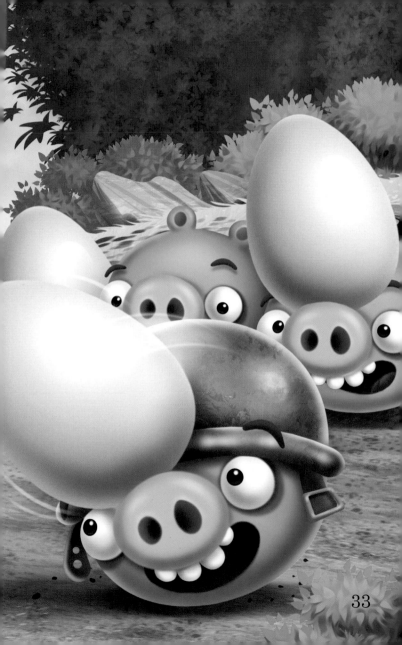

"You must go to the Evergreen Egg Tree," said the old pig. "There, you will be sure to find all the eggs you need!"

"The Evergreen Egg Tree! Wow!" said Corporal Pig. "But where is it?"

34

"For that, you must pay another egg!" said the old pig.

"That seems fair," thought Corporal Pig, and he did so.

"The tree grows right in the very middle of an icky swamp," said the stranger.

"That's no good!" cried Corporal Pig.
"We can't get to it there!"

The old pig laughed again.
"There is another way," she said.
"You could grow an Evergreen
Egg Tree of your own."

The old pig took something from her shawl. "This shoot comes from the Evergreen Egg Tree," she explained. "It will grow into another tree. You may have it – for just one more egg."

"Silly old things!" laughed Stella, as the pigs went on their way with the weed.

She set off for home to find the other birds and tell them all about her little trick – and to put all three eggs back in their nest.

43

And as for King Pig? Well, he was not as pleased with the Evergreen Egg Tree as Corporal Pig thought he would be...

How much do you remember about the story of Angry Birds: Stella and the Egg Tree? Answer these questions and find out!

- Who is in a bad mood at the beginning?

- How many eggs are stolen from the birds' nest?

- What does Stella disguise herself with?

- Where does Stella tell the pigs they will be able to find lots of eggs?

- What does she tell the pigs the weed is?

- How many eggs does Corporal Pig have for King Pig at the end?